# COOKING WITH
# 5 INGREDIENTS FROM

## *Trader Joe's*

## SIMPLE WEEKNIGHT MEALS
### Using Your Favorite In-Store Products

# COOKING WITH
# 5 INGREDIENTS FROM

*Trader Joe's*

## TRACEY KORSEN
### Founder of the Tracey Joe's blog

PAGE STREET
PUBLISHING CO.

PAGE STREET
PUBLISHING CO.

Copyright © 2021 Tracey Johnson

First published in 2021 by
Page Street Publishing Co.
27 Congress Street, Suite 1511
Salem, MA 01970
www.pagestreetpublishing.com

Distributed by Macmillan, sales in Canada by The Canadian Manda Group.

26   25   24            7   8   9

ISBN-13: 978-1-64567-390-3
ISBN-10: 1-64567-390-1

Library of Congress Control Number: 2021931372

Cover and book design by Meg Baskis for Page Street Publishing Co.
Photography by Toni Zernik

Printed and bound in the United States

*Dedication*

**TO DAVID**

# Contents

# Introduction

Hi, my name is Tracey (also known as @traceyjoes on Instagram). If you've been to my page, it may seem like I've always loved to cook and am naturally creative in the kitchen. This could not be further from the truth! I was first introduced to Trader Joe's in college, and my life was never the same. I mean, I practically lived off of the frozen chicken tikka masala my junior year. Their frozen meals also saved me when I entered grad school in 2015. As a PhD student, not having to think about complicated meals I needed to make when I got home from the library saved me from more than a few headaches. This all changed in the summer of 2019 when I rented a room from a family in New York City during a month-long research trip I took for my dissertation. Each night, the mom would make these amazing meals filled with herbs and spices that surely must have come from years and years of experience in the kitchen. One such meal was meatballs with a creamy tomato sauce and quinoa and roasted veggies topped with freshly minced dill. I asked her where everything was from and she said Trader Joe's. I. WAS. SHOOK! First, that this amazing meal amounted to the frozen turkey meatballs and creamy roasted tomato soup that I've always had on hand, but second, that my host creatively used them together with the dill to make a complex and delicious meal that took only about 30 minutes to make.

From then on I was committed to cooking creatively. I watched cooking shows like *Diners, Drive-Ins and Dives* and *Salt Fat Acid Heat* for inspiration, but put my Trader/ Tracey Joe's spin on the recipes I saw there. I soon learned that it is not difficult at all to make tasty, even restaurant-quality, meals at home using affordable ingredients from TJ's! I have compiled these recipes here for you in this book, and now you too can make delicious, one-of-a-kind meals with only a few ingredients.

Tracey Horsen

# Fridge and Pantry Staples

These are items I always have on hand and that I will expect you to also have as you make recipes from this book. These staples do not count toward the five-ingredient count! Yes, this may seem like cheating on my part, but these are items I bet you have in your refrigerator or pantry right now.

1. Salt, pepper and other basic dried seasonings
2. Flour
3. Broth
4. Oil
5. Butter

# Comfort Food

Ah, comfort food, my favorite food group. It's never quite one thing. One day it could be a PB & J at 2:00 a.m. while doomscrolling through Twitter. Another day, it could be meatloaf and mashed potatoes after work. While comfort food is definitely subjective, there are some universal qualities that make it what it is:

1. It's perfect on cold and/or rainy days.
2. It's creamy.
3. It's hearty.
4. It makes you feel good.

My favorites from this section are the One-Pot Orzo (page 23) and the BBQ Chicken Grilled Cheese (page 35).

# *Pulled* CHICKEN BBQ TACOS

Add a southern twist to your regular Taco Tuesday with this scrumptious recipe. The Organic Kansas City Style BBQ Sauce is hands down the best barbecue sauce (and possibly the best sauce, period) that Trader Joe's carries. Add some crunch with roasted corn and spiciness with pickled jalapeños.

**YIELD**: 8 tacos
**TOTAL TIME**: 30 minutes

## INGREDIENTS

**8 Trader Joe's Chicken Breast Tenderloins, defrosted**

2 tbsp (30 ml) olive oil

1–2 tsp (6–12 g) salt

1–2 tsp (2–4 g) pepper

**1 cup (154 g) Trader Joe's Roasted Corn**

**1 cup (240 ml) Trader Joe's Organic Kansas City Style BBQ Sauce**

**1 (15.5-oz [440-g]) package Trader Joe's Handmade Flour Tortillas**

**Trader Joe's Hot & Sweet Jalapeños, to serve**

## DIRECTIONS

Preheat the oven to 350°F (180°C).

Place the chicken tenderloins in a baking dish and drizzle them with the olive oil. Sprinkle with the salt and pepper. Bake for 25 minutes.

While the chicken cooks, heat the corn in a pot over medium heat for about 5 minutes. Set aside.

Once the chicken is cooked, shred it with two forks and mix in the BBQ sauce.

Heat up the tortillas by placing them, one at a time, on a dry pan over medium heat for 1 to 2 minutes per side.

Assemble the tacos by layering a tortilla with chicken, corn and jalapeño slices.

# *Buttermilk* BISCUIT CHICKEN POTPIE

If you were to look up "comfort food" in the dictionary, you would probably find a picture of a chicken potpie. This recipe is a no-fuss version that has a little bit of flair from the buttermilk biscuit topping.

**YIELD**: 4 servings
**TOTAL TIME**: 40 minutes

## INGREDIENTS

1 tbsp (15 ml) olive oil

**1 lb (454 g) Trader Joe's Chicken Breast Tenderloins, defrosted and cubed**

**1 cup (128 g) Trader Joe's Vegetable Melange**

1 cup (240 ml) Trader Joe's Organic Low Sodium Chicken Broth

**1 cup (240 ml) Trader Joe's Organic Whole Milk**

Salt and pepper, to taste

1 tsp dried thyme

2 tbsp (16 g) all-purpose flour

**1 (16-oz [454-g]) can Trader Joe's Buttermilk Biscuits**

## DIRECTIONS

Preheat the oven to 350°F (180°C).

Add the olive oil to a medium pot over medium heat. Add the chicken and stir occasionally until cooked through, 8 to 10 minutes.

Add the vegetable melange, chicken broth, milk, salt, pepper, thyme and flour to the pot, and stir to thicken the potpie mixture. Once the sauce has thickened, about 5 minutes, add the mixture to a 8 x 8 x 2–inch (20 x 20 x 5–cm) baking dish.

Open the buttermilk biscuits and place them on top of the potpie mixture. Bake uncovered for 25 minutes on the middle rack to ensure the biscuits cook but the tops don't burn. Tops should be slightly darker than golden brown. Let cool for 5 minutes before serving.

# *Black Bean Soup* WITH CHIMICHURRI RICE AND JALAPEÑO SAUSAGE

I was a late bloomer when it came to trying the frozen rice from Trader Joe's, which means I somehow did not even realize it existed until 2020. DON'T JUDGE ME! I get tunnel vision when I go into TJ's, and I will not apologize for it. But now that I have tried all the frozen rice they have to offer, I must say, the chimichurri rice is probably my favorite. So, why not add it to one of my favorite food groups: soup! This recipe cooks up quickly and is quite comforting while also packing a punch with a little bit of spice from the rice.

**YIELD**: 6 servings
**TOTAL TIME**: 20 minutes

## INGREDIENTS

1 tbsp (15 ml) olive oil

1 (12-oz [340-g]) package Trader Joe's Spicy Jalapeño Chicken Sausage, sliced

1 (16-oz [454-g]) bag Trader Joe's Peruvian Style Chimichurri Rice with Vegetables

1 (32-oz [946-ml]) container Trader Joe's Latin Style Black Bean Soup

Salt and pepper, to taste

1 (9-oz [255-g]) bag Trader Joe's Restaurant Style White Corn Tortilla Chips

Trader Joe's Organic Sour Cream, to serve

## DIRECTIONS

Place a heavy-bottomed pot over medium heat and coat with the olive oil.

Add the sausage slices and cook until browned on both sides, about 3 minutes.

Add the chimichurri rice and cook, stirring occasionally for about 5 minutes.

Add the black bean soup and let it come to a simmer. Add salt and pepper to taste.

Ladle the soup into six bowls, and add three to four chips and a dollop of sour cream to each serving.

# *One-Pot* ORZO

This One-Pot Orzo is one of my most popular recipes. I did not realize how much people loved orzo, but truly, what's not to love? It's a tiny, versatile pasta that's perfect warm or cold. But, you want to serve this recipe warm. This recipe is filling and leaves almost zero mess because, as its name would suggest, it's made in one pot!

**YIELD**: 4 servings
**TOTAL TIME**: 25 minutes

## INGREDIENTS

1 tbsp (15 ml) olive oil

**1 (12-oz [340-g]) package Trader Joe's Sun-Dried Tomato Chicken Sausage, sliced**

**1 (12-oz [340-g]) package fresh asparagus, chopped**

**1 bell pepper, sliced**

**½ yellow onion, diced**

**1 cup (210 g) Trader Joe's Authentic Imported Italian Orzo Pasta**

Salt and pepper, to taste

## DIRECTIONS

Place a heavy-bottomed pot over medium-high heat and coat with the olive oil.

Add the sausage and brown on both sides, about 3 minutes.

Add the asparagus, bell pepper and onion and sauté for about 5 minutes.

Add the orzo and 2 cups (480 ml) of water to the pot. Stir the mixture continuously until the orzo is cooked completely through, 12 to 15 minutes. Add more liquid if you need it. When ready, add salt and pepper to taste before serving.

# NO-WINE TURKEY BOLOGNESE

If you don't have time to make a classic, slow-simmered bolognese, the "Just Sauce" Turkey Bolognese from Trader Joe's is the perfect alternative. I like to jazz it up by adding garlic, an orange peel and a bit of soy sauce (trust me) to mimic the depth of the traditional slow-cooked sauce.

**YIELD**: 3 servings
**TOTAL TIME**: 35 minutes

## INGREDIENTS

1 tbsp (15 ml) olive oil

**2 tsp (6 g) minced garlic**

**1 (12-oz [340-g]) package Trader Joe's "Just Sauce" Turkey Bolognese**

**1 tbsp (15 ml) soy sauce**

**1" (2.5-cm) square piece orange peel**

**1 (16-oz [454-g]) bag Trader Joe's Italian Rigatoni**

## DIRECTIONS

Place a heavy-bottomed pot over medium heat and coat with the olive oil. Add the garlic and stir frequently, making sure it doesn't burn. Cook until fragrant, about 3 minutes.

Add the turkey bolognese and stir. Add the soy sauce and orange peel and let it simmer for 30 minutes.

While the bolognese is simmering, cook the rigatoni according to the package's instructions.

When the pasta is done, use a large slotted spoon to add it to the bolognese sauce. I don't like to drain my pasta completely because the excess pasta water helps to thicken up the sauce. Mix well. Remove the orange peel, then serve.

# SHRIMP AND BROCCOLI
## *Alfredo*

One of my favorite restaurant meals (from a certain seafood chain with the famous cheddar bay biscuits) is shrimp and broccoli Alfredo. Obviously, going to restaurants all the time isn't good for your budget, so, when my mom started making this for our family on the weekdays, I remember thinking, oh, we're FAAANCY! Give yourself and your family that same feeling by making this version! Trader Joe's Fettuccine Alfredo is easy to make and is creamy and luxurious . . . unlike other brands I've tried. I suggest cooking two bags if you're feeding more than two people.

**YIELD**: 4 servings
**TOTAL TIME**: 10 minutes

### INGREDIENTS

2 (16-oz [454-g]) bags Trader Giotto's Fettuccine Alfredo

2 cups (182 g) Trader Joe's Broccoli Florets

2 cups (650 g) Trader Joe's Medium Cooked Shrimp

Trader Joe's Parmesan Cheese Grated, to serve

### DIRECTIONS

Place a large pot over medium heat. Add 4 tablespoons (60 ml) of water, both packages of fettuccine, the broccoli and shrimp. Cook covered for 2 minutes.

Remove the lid and stir the sauce to incorporate all of the ingredients. Cover the pot and cook until heated through, at least 5 minutes.

Serve with the grated Parmesan.

# *Tater Tot* CASSEROLE

This meal is an ode to my Minnesotan mother-in-law who has told me many stories about the hearty dishes she grew up eating during the harsh winters. I decided to pass on attempting the seven-layer salad (which her two sons would say are just seven layers of mayonnaise) and went straight to the tater tot casserole. And it was definitely for the best. I mean, you can't go wrong with tater tots and cheese, people.

**YIELD**: 6 servings
**TOTAL TIME**: 45 minutes

### INGREDIENTS

**1 lb (454 g) ground beef**

**2 cups (256 g) Trader Joe's Vegetable Melange**

**1 (11-oz [312-g]) container Trader Joe's Condensed Cream of Portabella Mushroom Soup**

**2 cups (226 g) Trader Joe's Shredded Cheddar Cheese**

**1 (2-lb [32-oz]) bag Trader Joe's Trader Potato Tots**

### DIRECTIONS

Preheat the oven to 450°F (230°C). Grease an 8 x 8 x 2–inch (20 x 20 x 5–cm) baking dish.

Cook the ground beef in a pan over medium heat until cooked through, about 10 minutes.

Add the vegetable melange and portabella mushroom soup. Stir to combine.

Add the mixture to the prepared baking dish. Top with the shredded cheese and a layer of potato tots.

Bake uncovered until heated through, about 30 minutes.

# *Creamy* SLOW COOKER RAVIOLI SOUP

My grad-school-roommate-turned-best-friend used to make this all the time. As I said in the introduction, I taught myself how to cook within the last few years, but when I got to grad school, all I could make without calling my mom for help was roasted vegetables. So, my girl Pam had my back and would oftentimes meal prep for the both of us. This soup is so comforting and surprisingly complex as you get creaminess from the cream cheese, savoriness from the sausage and a slight hit of acid from the tomatoes. Make this soup and have meals for days!

**YIELD**: 6 servings
**TOTAL TIME**: 3–7 hours (depending on your slow cooker settings)

## INGREDIENTS

1 (16-oz [454-g]) package Trader Joe's Sweet Italian Pork Sausage

1 (12-oz [355-ml]) container Trader Joe's Organic Low Sodium Chicken Broth

1 (16-oz [454-g]) bag Trader Joe's Mini Ravioli with Cheese Filling

1 (8-oz [227-g]) block Trader Joe's Cream Cheese

1 (14.5-oz [411-g]) can Trader Joe's Organic Tomatoes Diced & Fire Roasted

## DIRECTIONS

Squeeze the sausages out of their casings and brown in a skillet over medium-high heat for 5 to 7 minutes. There's no need to add oil as the fat from the sausage provides enough oil.

Drain the fat and add the sausages to a large crockpot along with the broth, ravioli, cream cheese and tomatoes. Stir the mixture together with a spoon.

Cook on low for 7 hours or on high for 3 hours.

# *BBQ* CHICKEN GRILLED CHEESE

While I love a classic grilled cheese, this BBQ version is perfect to help you switch things up every now and then. It's especially great because it keeps you fuller longer because of the protein from the chicken.

**YIELD**: 2 sandwiches
**TOTAL TIME**: 45 minutes

## INGREDIENTS

6 Trader Joe's Chicken Tenderloins, defrosted

1 cup (240 ml) Trader Joe's Organic Kansas Style BBQ Sauce

2 slices Trader Joe's Sliced Colby Jack Cheese

4 slices Trader Joe's Sourdough Bread

1 tbsp (14 g) butter

## DIRECTIONS

Preheat the oven to 350°F (180°C).

Place the chicken in a baking dish and bake until cooked, about 25 minutes.

Pull the chicken apart with two forks. Add it to a small pot over medium-low heat and add the BBQ sauce. Stir to combine. Let it warm up for about 3 minutes.

Assemble the grilled cheese by placing 1 slice of Colby Jack cheese on one side of the bread, place half the BBQ chicken on top of the cheese and then place the second slice of bread on top of the chicken. Repeat for the second sandwich.

Place a saucepan over medium heat, and add the butter. Once the butter begins to bubble, place one of the sandwiches in the pan until the bread becomes golden and crispy on both sides, about 3 minutes per side. Repeat with the second sandwich.

# Takeout, but Make It Trader Joe's

I love takeout and I love restaurant classics. As a person who didn't learn to cook for themselves for a while—and who constantly ordered food from corner spots—that kind of food is near and dear to me. But, as a graduate student living on a budget, I had to learn how to make these delicious creations on my own. This turned out to be better for my wallet and my waistline, as I was able make more appropriate portions for myself. Win-win! Make sure to check out the Easy Gyros with Pita (page 53) and the British-Style Fish 'n' Chips (page 47)!

# *Brooklyn* BANGERS + PEPPERS

Can't get to a biergarten for a brat and a beer? No worries! Enter these Brooklyn bangers. I love these for many reasons, but mostly because they have yummy, melty cheese inside. *Enter drooling face emoji here.*

**YIELD**: 4 servings
**TOTAL TIME**: 35 minutes

## INGREDIENTS

2 tbsp (30 ml) olive oil, divided

**1 (16-oz [454-g]) package Brooklyn Bangers Cheddar Bratwurst**

**1 red bell pepper, sliced**

**1 sweet onion, sliced**

Salt and pepper, to taste

4 tbsp (57 g) butter

**4 Trader Joe's Hot Dog Buns**

**Trader Joe's Deli Style Spicy Brown Mustard, to serve**

## DIRECTIONS

Pour 1 tablespoon (15 ml) of the oil into a large saucepan over medium heat. Once the oil is hot, place the Brooklyn bangers in the pan and cook for 5 minutes per side.

Pour the remaining oil into a small saucepan over medium heat, and add the bell pepper, onion, salt and pepper. Stir occasionally until the veggies soften and even get a bit charred, about 10 minutes.

Pour about 2 tablespoons (30 ml) of water into the pan with the bangers and cover for 3 to 5 minutes. I do this because the sausages are thick, and there is cheese in the middle, so I want to be sure it cooks all the way through and the cheese gets nice and melty.

While the bangers are finishing cooking, butter the hot dog buns and place on a foil-lined baking sheet. Broil until browned, 3 to 5 minutes.

Take the buns out of the oven, and begin to assemble the bangers by dividing everything among the buns. Place a sausage in a bun, add some of the onion and bell pepper and top with a squeeze of spicy brown mustard.

# *Philly* CHEESESTEAKS

When my husband and I first moved to Philadelphia, we vowed to find the best cheesesteak in the city. In order to achieve this goal, we instituted Cheesesteak Sundays and would visit one to two cheesesteak joints each Sunday and grade them. After a while, we felt confident that we could probably make our own delicious version, and we did! While many people might add mayo, lettuce or sautéed mushrooms to their cheesesteak, the classic way to have it is "wit wiz" (meaning with Cheese Whiz) and grilled onions. (In this recipe, we use Trader Joe's Pub Cheese, which is a great alternative.) Try this recipe and immediately transport yourself to the City of Brotherly Love.

**YIELD**: 4 sandwiches
**TOTAL TIME**: 30 minutes

## INGREDIENTS

2 tbsp (30 ml) olive oil, divided

**1 (16-oz [454-g]) package Trader Joe's All Natural Shaved Beef Steak**

1 tsp salt, plus more if desired

1 tsp pepper, plus more if desired

**½ white or yellow onion, diced**

**1 (8-oz [227-g]) Trader Joe's Sharp Cheddar Pub Cheese**

**1 Trader Joe's Organic French Baguette**

(continued)

# *Philly* CHEESESTEAKS (CONTINUED)

## DIRECTIONS

Pour 1 tablespoon (15 ml) of the oil in a large saucepan over medium heat. Separate the shaved beef steak with your hands and add it to the hot pan. Season the beef with the salt and pepper. Be careful not to add too much salt since you'll be adding pub cheese, which is quite salty.

Once the meat is cooked through, 5 to 7 minutes, remove it from the pan and place on a plate. Add the remaining oil and the onion to the pan. Add more salt and pepper, if desired, and cook until the onion is translucent, about 5 minutes.

Heat the pub cheese in a saucepan over medium-low heat for 5 to 10 minutes or by placing it in the microwave for 2 minutes.

Cut your baguette in half lengthwise and put in the oven on broil for 5 minutes.

Your cheesesteak is ready to be assembled! Layer the shaved beef steak, pub cheese and onion on the baguette and cut into four sandwiches.

# *British-Style* FISH 'N' CHIPS

If a restaurant has fish 'n' chips on the menu, I am getting it! It has always been (and always will be) one of my favorite meals. There's just something so wonderful about perfectly battered and fried fish that truly makes me happy. Oh, and french fries, of course. Now you can have that experience from home using Trader Joe's ridiculously delicious battered halibut.

**YIELD**: 3 servings
**TOTAL TIME**: 30 minutes

## INGREDIENTS

**1 (1½-lb [680-g]) package Trader Joe's Potato Fries**

1 tbsp (18 g) salt

**2 cups (268 g) Trader Joe's Petite Peas**

1 cup (240 ml) vegetable oil

**1 (10-oz [284-g]) package Trader Joe's Battered Halibut**

**3 tbsp (45 ml) Trader Joe's Tartar Sauce**

**1 lemon, sliced into wedges**

## DIRECTIONS

Preheat the oven to 425°F (220°C). Lightly coat a baking sheet with nonstick cooking spray.

Arrange the fries in a single layer on the baking sheet. Bake for 14 minutes.

Pour 2 cups (480 ml) of water into a pot and add the salt. Over high heat, let the water come to a boil, and then add the peas. Cook for 5 minutes. Drain the peas, mash them with a potato masher and set side.

To deep-fry the halibut, heat the vegetable oil in a large cast-iron skillet. Add the fish and fry until brown, about 3 minutes per side.

Assemble the fish 'n' chips by placing the french fries, halibut and peas on a plate. Serve with tartar sauce and lemon wedges.

# *Carne Asada* QUESADILLAS

This meal is so good that you won't believe it only takes twenty minutes to make. Trader Joe's does most of the work for you with this deliciously marinated and thinly cut carne asada. It cooks through in minutes, and while you're letting the meat rest, you can get the rest of the ingredients together quick as can be!

**YIELD**: 4 quesadillas
**TOTAL TIME**: 20 minutes

## INGREDIENTS

1 tbsp (15 ml) olive oil

1 (16-oz [454-g]) package Trader Joe's Carne Asada Autentica

4 tbsp (61 g) Trader Joe's Fat Free Refried Beans

8 Trader Joe's Handmade Flour Tortillas

1 (12-oz [340-g]) package Trader Joe's Fancy Shredded Mexican Style Cheese Blend

8 tbsp (124 g) Trader Joe's Mild Pico de Gallo Salsa

## DIRECTIONS

Pour the oil in a saucepan over medium-high heat. Add the carne asada, and cook for 3 to 4 minutes on each side. Remove the carne asada, and place on a cutting block to rest for 5 minutes before slicing into strips.

Assemble each quesadilla by placing 1 tablespoon (15 g) of refried beans on a tortilla and spreading it around with a spoon or spatula. For each quesadilla, sprinkle ¼ to ½ cup (28 to 46 g) of cheese, place six to ten strips of carne asada on top and pour on 2 tablespoons (31 g) of salsa. Then, place another tortilla on top.

In a skillet over medium heat, brown each side of the quesadilla for 1 to 2 minutes per side. Repeat for each quesadilla.

# *Easy* GYROS WITH PITA

I don't think I can emphasize enough how good the gyro slices from TJ's are. This gyro pita is second only to getting the real thing from someone who's been making it their whole life—I KID YOU NOT! This meal is doubly perfect because you can assemble them in fifteen minutes!

**YIELD**: 2 servings
**TOTAL TIME**: 15 minutes

## INGREDIENTS

**1 (8-oz [227-g]) package Trader Joe's Gyro Slices**

**¼ red onion**

**2 Roma tomatoes**

**2 Trader Joe's Pita Bread Pockets**

**½ cup (120 g) Trader Joe's Tzatziki Creamy Garlic Cucumber Dip**

## DIRECTIONS

Cook the gyro slices in a large saucepan over medium heat until they become dark brown, about 10 minutes.

While the gyro slices are cooking, prepare the vegetables by slicing the onion and tomatoes widthwise.

When the gyro slices are cooked, assemble the pitas like you would a taco. Divide each of the ingredients between the two pita pockets by layering the tomato, onion and gyro slices inside, and then drizzling the tzatziki on top.

# New Orleans-Inspired
# SHRIMP PO'BOYS

A couple of years ago, I took my first trip to New Orleans as an adult. While the music, drinks and parties are great, the food is simply spectacular. My husband and I had multiple po'boys on our three-day trip—oyster po'boys, surf 'n' turf po'boys, shrimp po'boys! This recipe brings me back to that sunny and delicious vacation.

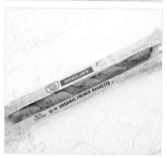

**YIELD**: 4 sandwiches
**TOTAL TIME**: 20 minutes

### INGREDIENTS

1 (16-oz [454-g]) package Trader Joe's Tempura Shrimp

1 Better Boy tomato, sliced

Salt and pepper, to taste

1 Trader Joe's Organic French Baguette

1 head iceberg lettuce, chopped

¼ cup (60 ml) Trader Joe's Magnifisauce

### DIRECTIONS

Preheat the oven to 400°F (200°C).

Arrange the frozen shrimp in a single layer on a baking sheet so they are not touching, and place the baking sheet on the middle rack of the oven. Bake for 8 to 10 minutes per side.

While the shrimp are cooking, lightly season the tomato with salt and pepper.

When the shrimp are cooked, use a knife to cut their tails off. Cut your baguette in half lengthwise.

Assemble your first po'boy by putting lettuce inside the baguette. Add the tomato slices, then the shrimp, and lastly the Magnifisauce. Repeat with the remaining ingredients. Cut the baguette into four sandwiches and serve.

# Fancy-ish Fare

The meals featured in this section are based on meals I've had at restaurants that I never thought I could make myself—mostly because professional chefs have a way of dreaming up recipes that include ingredients that we regular people may not have thought to pair together. While I do consider the recipes in this chapter "fancy," I want to emphasize the "ish" so you're not too intimidated. These meals are still fairly easy to make and contain lots of depth that will surely impress you, your family and your friends. A few of my favorites include the Harissa Meatballs (page 67) and the Pesto Chicken and Spaghetti with Soffritto Seasoning (page 73).

# *Vegetarian* GYOZA CURRY

This soup brings together two of my favorite TJ's products: the vegetable gyoza and the Thai red curry sauce. Initially, I had used the curry solely to marinate meat, but I decided to explore beyond my horizons and start using it in soups and stews. And voilà, this recipe was born! It's savory, slightly tangy and surprisingly filling.

**YIELD**: 3 servings
**TOTAL TIME**: 20 minutes

## INGREDIENTS

3 tbsp (45 ml) olive oil, divided

**½ red onion, diced**

1 tsp salt

1 tsp pepper

**1 cup (240 ml) Trader Joe's Thai Style Red Curry Sauce**

1½ cups (360 ml) Trader Joe's Organic Low Sodium Vegetable Broth

**1 cup (150 g) Trader Joe's Green Vegetable Foursome**

**1 (16-oz [454-g]) package Trader Joe's Thai Vegetable Gyoza**

## DIRECTIONS

Add 1 tablespoon (15 ml) of the oil to a medium saucepan over medium heat. Add the onion, salt and pepper. Stir with a spatula until the onion becomes translucent, about 5 minutes.

Add the Thai red curry sauce and vegetable broth and stir. Let it come to a simmer, about 3 minutes, and then add the vegetables. Place a lid on top, and turn the heat to low while you cook the gyoza.

Panfry the gyoza by heating the remaining oil in a sauté pan over medium heat. Place the frozen gyoza flat side down in the pan and sauté until they turn lightly brown, about 4 minutes. Reduce the heat to medium-low, and carefully add 3 to 4 tablespoons (45 to 60 ml) of water to the pan and cover it immediately.

Steam the gyoza until the water has evaporated, 5 to 6 minutes.

To serve, ladle the soup into three bowls, and add gyoza to each.

# *Creole* SCALLOPS AND GRITS

Scallops are my favorite seafood and are something that I only used to eat in restaurants because they seemed intimidating to cook. I could not have been further from the truth! The wild fresh sea scallops at Trader Joe's are great quality, and when cooked correctly, they are buttery and so tasty. Quickly assemble a creole seasoning, coat both sides of your scallops and sear them for a couple of minutes in a hot, well-oiled pan and you'll have perfectly delicious scallops. This take on the traditional shrimp and grits is a must-try.

**YIELD**: Approximately 4 servings
**TOTAL TIME**: 30 minutes

## INGREDIENTS

1¼ tsp (8 g) salt, divided

1 tsp pepper

1 tsp garlic powder

1 tsp smoked paprika

1 tsp oregano

1 tsp dried thyme

1 tsp cayenne

1 tbsp (14 g) butter

**½ cup (78 g) Trader Joe's Stone Ground White Grits**

**½ cup (120 ml) milk**

2 tbsp (30 ml) olive oil, divided

**1 (16-oz [454-g]) package Trader Joe's Wild Fresh Sea Scallops**

**1 red bell pepper, sliced**

**½ sweet onion, sliced**

(continued)

## DIRECTIONS

To make the creole seasoning, in a bowl, mix together 1 teaspoon of salt, the pepper, garlic powder, smoked paprika, oregano, thyme and cayenne and set aside.

In a large pot, combine 1½ cups (360 ml) of water, the remaining salt and butter, and bring to a boil. Gradually stir in the grits and let the water return to a boil. Lower the heat as low as possible. Cook covered, stirring frequently for 15 to 20 minutes. Add the milk and stir for 10 minutes, or until all the liquid is absorbed.

While the grits are cooking, place a sauté pan over medium-high heat, and add 1 tablespoon (15 ml) of the olive oil. Pat the scallops dry and season them with the creole seasoning mixture. When the oil is hot, add the scallops flat side down and cook no more than five at a time for 3 minutes on each side.

When the scallops are finished cooking, put them aside and use the same pan to sauté the bell pepper and onion along with the remaining oil. Stir occasionally with a spatula until soft, about 5 minutes.

When the grits are finished, divide them among four bowls, then add the onion and bell pepper and two to three scallops per bowl.

# SOY CHORIZO AND BRUSSELS SPROUTS *Hash*

The best thing about this recipe is that you can feel good about the fact that there are Brussels sprouts in here even though you can't taste them AT ALL! Therefore, this is a perfect meal to sneak in veggies for kids (or adults, let's be real) who might not be eating their fair share of the green stuff.

**YIELD**: 2 servings
**TOTAL TIME**: 30 minutes

## INGREDIENTS

**2 cups (283 g) Trader Joe's Trader Potato Tots**

**1 (12-oz [340-g]) package Trader Joe's Soy Chorizo**

**1 cup (88 g) Brussels sprouts**

2 tsp (10 ml) vegetable oil

**2 eggs**

**¼ cup (60 g) Trader Joe's Salsa Especial**

## DIRECTIONS

Preheat the oven to 400°F (200°C). Line a baking sheet with aluminum foil.

Place the potato tots in a single layer on the baking sheet. Bake for 20 minutes, flipping halfway through. Set aside.

Place a large, oven-safe skillet over medium heat. Add the soy chorizo to the skillet and use a spatula to crumble the chorizo.

Slice the Brussels sprouts in half and then into strips. Add to the skillet and cook the chorizo and Brussels sprouts for 5 minutes.

With the spatula, create two holes in the soy chorizo mixture. Pour 1 teaspoon of vegetable oil into each hole, and then crack an egg into each hole. Place the skillet in the oven until the eggs have set, 5 to 7 minutes.

Take the chorizo-and-egg mixture out of the oven and top with the potato tots and salsa.

# *Harissa* MEATBALLS

I'll be honest with you: I never had harissa until I tried it from Trader Joe's. But once I did, it kind of changed my life! It's spicy but not too spicy. (Trust me, I'm super-sensitive to spices. I've dealt with heartburn since I was five, because apparently, I've always been an old person in a young person's body.) It gives your food wonderful warmth and depth of flavor. It's perfect in these meatballs and makes enough for meal prep or for a small gathering. Serve with toasted sourdough or jasmine rice.

**YIELD**: About 24 meatballs
**TOTAL TIME**: 45 minutes

## INGREDIENTS

**1 lb (454 g) ground beef**

**1 lb (454 g) ground pork**

**1–2 tbsp (21–42 g) Trader Joe's Traditional Tunisian Harissa Hot Chili Pepper Paste with Herbs & Spices**

**2 eggs**

**¼ cup (40 g) Trader Joe's Organic Bread Crumbs**

2 tsp (12 g) salt

2 tsp (4 g) pepper

1 tbsp (15 ml) olive oil

(continued)

# *Harissa* MEATBALLS (CONTINUED)

## DIRECTIONS

Preheat the oven to 350°F (180°C). Line a baking sheet with aluminum foil and grease the foil.

In a bowl, add the ground beef, ground pork, harissa paste, eggs, bread crumbs, salt and pepper. Combine all of the ingredients with your hands.

Place a heavy-bottomed pot over medium heat and add the olive oil.

At this point, I like to take about a 1-teaspoon-size ball of meat and cook it on its own so I can test for seasoning. Once you try it, you can decide if you need more harissa, salt, etc.

Use a 1-inch (2.5-cm) cookie scoop to make golf ball–sized meatballs, and sear the meatballs on all sides to get them nice and brown, about 3 minutes on each side. Cook in batches of about six meatballs.

Once browned, place the meatballs on the baking sheet. Bake for 12 to 15 minutes.

# *Mini* FRENCH BAGUETTES AND SPICY HONEY RICOTTA DIP

This is a perfect recipe if you want something easy to make before you have guests over! The spicy honey gives you the sweet and the heat but is also cool and creamy from the whipped ricotta. Trader Joe's Mini French Baguettes are a wonderful item to whip up for events big and small because they allow people to easily dip their bread in this sweet, savory and spicy dip.

**YIELD**: 3 servings
**TOTAL TIME**: 15 minutes

## INGREDIENTS

1 (9.5-oz [270-g]) package Trader Joe's Mini French Baguettes

½ cup (120 ml) Trader Joe's Honey

2 tsp (7 g) crushed red pepper flakes

1 (16-oz [454-g]) container Trader Joe's Whole Milk or Part Skim Ricotta Cheese

1 tsp fresh thyme

(continued)

# *Mini* FRENCH BAGUETTES AND SPICY HONEY RICOTTA DIP (CONTINUED)

## DIRECTIONS

Preheat the oven to 400°F (200°C).

Remove the baguettes from the packaging and place them directly on an oven rack. Bake for 12 minutes. The directions say 6 minutes, but they are still quite doughy inside when only cooked for that long.

While the baguettes are cooking, place a saucepan over medium heat, and add the honey and crushed red pepper flakes. Simmer for 5 minutes, stirring occasionally. Remove from the heat and let it come to room temperature.

Pour the honey through a fine-mesh sieve and into a mixing bowl. Add the ricotta and fresh thyme, and mix with an electric mixer until the ricotta becomes fluffy, about 5 minutes.

Add the mixture to a serving bowl and use the baguettes to dip.

# *Pesto* CHICKEN AND SPAGHETTI WITH SOFFRITTO SEASONING

I have always been a fan of the pesto chicken from Trader Joe's, but it is elevated to new heights when you add soffritto seasoning to it! This meal cooks up in just 25 minutes and makes four large servings.

**YIELD**: 4 servings
**TOTAL TIME**: 25 minutes

## INGREDIENTS

2 tbsp (36 g) salt

**1 (16-oz [454-g]) package Trader Joe's Italian Spaghetti**

6 tbsp (90 ml) olive oil, divided

**1 (16-oz [454-g]) package Trader Joe's Pesto Genovese Chicken Breast**

**1 cup (150 g) sliced cherry tomatoes**

**2 tbsp (12 g) Trader Joe's Italian Style Soffritto Seasoning Blend**

## DIRECTIONS

In a large pot, bring 4 quarts (4 L) of water to a boil. Add the salt and spaghetti and boil for 8 minutes, stirring frequently.

While the spaghetti is cooking, place a large saucepan over medium-high heat and add 2 tablespoons (30 ml) of the olive oil. Once the oil is hot, add the pesto chicken, cooking for 5 minutes on each side. Take the chicken out of the pan, place it on a plate and set aside.

When the pasta is done, add 1 cup (240 ml) of cold water to stop the cooking, drain and add the spaghetti to the pan where you cooked the chicken. Add the cherry tomatoes, soffritto and remaining olive oil and toss.

Add the chicken to the spaghetti, toss and serve.

# *Pesto* CHICKEN AND SPAGHETTI WITH SOFFRITTO SEASONING (CONTINUED)

# Mostly Healthy

Like most people, I go through phases of healthy eating and eating a lot of "junk." Before my wedding, I did a strict "no-processed carbs" diet for two months. During peak dissertation writing, I ate any and every piece of bread and pasta in sight. Such is life, folks! This section is for those times when you need fewer processed foods and more whole ingredients in your life. Oh, did I mention they all taste delicious? My favorites include the Chicken Salsa Verde Soup (page 91) and the One-Pan Chicken Legs (page 79).

# *One-Pan* CHICKEN LEGS

Drumsticks are my favorite part of the chicken, so we make this meal in my household a lot! This recipe is very customizable; you can use almost any root veggie if you're not a carrot fan. (I've used both potatoes and butternut squash before.) Also, I love to switch up the seasonings. Sometimes I do the classic salt and pepper, and other times, I love to mix it up with curry powder! Don't let the cooking time scare you, as once you pop these babies in the oven, you don't even have to think about them, and they come out perfectly! Also, don't let the amount of olive oil scare you. The entire bottle is used to ensure the juiciest, most tender chicken drumsticks ever. You won't be spending tons of money, either, as Trader Joe's Organic Extra Virgin Olive Oil sells for a fraction of the price of olive oil in most other grocery stores.

**YIELD**: 2 servings
**TOTAL TIME**: 1½–2 hours

## INGREDIENTS

2–4 Trader Joe's All Natural Chicken Drumsticks

5 whole organic carrots, peeled

1 yellow onion, quartered

2 shallots, halved

1 (16.9-oz [500-ml]) bottle Trader Joe's Organic Extra Virgin Olive Oil Mediterranean Blend

2 tsp (12 g) salt

2 tsp (4 g) pepper

## DIRECTIONS

Preheat the oven to 325°F (165°C).

Place the drumsticks, carrots, onion and shallots in a 9 x 13–inch (23 x 33–cm) baking dish.

Pour the entire jar of olive oil over the chicken and into the baking dish and add the salt and pepper. Reserve 2 tablespoons (30 ml) of the oil if you want crispy skin.

Place the baking dish in the oven and bake for 1½ hours. Pierce a chicken leg with a fork to see if the meat is tough or if it easily falls apart. If it is still quite tough, leave it in for 30 more minutes.

If you like your chicken legs to have crispy skin, add 2 tablespoons (30 ml) of the olive oil to a pan over medium heat, and brown the skins for 3 to 5 minutes. This will not overcook the chicken.

# *Simple* CHICKEN ENCHILADAS WITH JICAMA WRAPS

Here's another low-carb recipe for you that is sure to please everyone! Baking the jicama wraps might be the best way to cook them because it takes some of the crunchiness out without shrinking them like when you cook them in a pan.

**YIELD**: 4 servings
**TOTAL TIME**: 45 minutes

## INGREDIENTS

6 frozen Trader Joe's Chicken Tenderloins, defrosted

1 tsp salt

1 tsp pepper

1 cup (240 ml) plus 1 tbsp (15 ml) Trader Joe's Enchilada Sauce, divided

1 (7.48-oz [212-g]) package Trader Joe's Jicama Wraps

1 cup (113 g) Trader Joe's Fancy Shredded Mexican Style Cheese Blend

## DIRECTIONS

Preheat the oven to 350°F (180°C).

Add the tenderloins to a 9 x 13–inch (23 x 33–cm) baking dish and sprinkle with the salt and pepper. Bake until the chicken is cooked, about 25 minutes.

Place the chicken in a large bowl, and shred the chicken with two forks.

Spread 1 tablespoon (15 ml) of the enchilada sauce on the bottom of a medium-sized baking dish.

Assemble the enchiladas by taking a jicama wrap and placing the shredded chicken (2 to 3 tablespoons [30 to 45 g] for each shell) in the middle. Fold the wrap on both sides so it looks like a cylinder, and then put the enchilada in the baking dish folded side down. Repeat until you've used all of the wraps and/or chicken.

Top the enchiladas with the remaining enchilada sauce and the shredded cheese. Bake for 20 minutes.

# *Low-Carb* RAMEN WITH PORK BELLY

Let's face it—ramen is hot right now! It's been hot for a few years, and it's going to be hot for the foreseeable future! I crave ramen on the regular, but when I was trying to fit into my wedding dress, I had to come up with a lighter option. Thank goodness Trader Joe's came out with the Hearts of Palm Pasta the summer before my wedding. Now you can make your own version of ramen with fewer carbs at home!

**YIELD**: 3 servings
**TOTAL TIME**: 30 minutes

## INGREDIENTS

**3 eggs**

**1 (12-oz [340-g]) box Trader Joe's Fully Cooked Pork Belly, sliced**

**1 cup (70 g) shiitake mushrooms**

1 tsp salt, plus a pinch

1 tsp pepper

1 tsp garlic powder

**1 (9-oz [255-g]) box Trader Joe's Hearts of Palm Pasta**

1 (12-oz [355-ml]) container Trader Joe's Organic Low Sodium Chicken Broth

(continued)

## DIRECTIONS

Fill a small pot with water and bring it to a boil. Carefully drop in the eggs and boil for 7 minutes. Place the hardboiled eggs in an ice bath for 5 minutes before peeling and setting aside.

Place a skillet over medium heat. Once hot, add the pork belly and panfry until brown on both sides, about 5 minutes per side. Remove the pork belly from the pan and set aside.

In the same pan, cook the mushrooms over medium heat for 5 minutes and season with the salt, pepper and garlic powder.

Place a medium-sized nonstick pot over medium heat and add the heart of palm pasta. I've made this pasta many times, and I have found that cooking it in a nonstick pot with no oil or water first helps take away some of the crunchy texture. Add a pinch of salt and cook for 5 minutes. Add the chicken broth and let it come to a simmer before assembling.

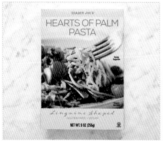

Assemble the ramen by dividing the hearts of palm pasta and broth among three bowls. Add a couple of slices of pork belly, an egg (halved) and a few shiitake mushrooms to each bowl.

# *Spaghetti Squash* WITH TRADER JOE'S VEGAN BOLOGNESE STYLE PASTA SAUCE

Isn't spaghetti squash amazing? I mean, really! Unlike cauliflower rice and cauliflower steaks, this is a vegetable that perfectly mimics the carb it's supposed to replace. It's like an angel hair pasta! And if I'm being honest, I actually like it better. Top it with Trader Joe's Vegan Bolognese Style Pasta Sauce, which is truly so good you can barely tell it's not meat!

**YIELD**: 4 servings
**TOTAL TIME**: 45 minutes

### INGREDIENTS

1 tbsp (15 ml) avocado oil

1 medium spaghetti squash, halved and de-seeded

Salt and pepper, as desired

2 cups (480 ml) Trader Joe's Vegan Bolognese Style Pasta Sauce

Fresh parsley, minced

(continued)

# *Spaghetti Squash* WITH TRADER JOE'S VEGAN BOLOGNESE STYLE PASTA SAUCE (CONTINUED)

## DIRECTIONS

Preheat the oven to 400°F (200°C). Line a baking sheet with aluminum foil.

Drizzle the oil on the inside of both halves of the spaghetti squash and sprinkle them with a little salt and pepper. Place both halves on the baking sheet inside side down and bake for 40 minutes.

About 10 minutes before the squash halves are done, add the sauce to a medium-sized pot and place over medium heat for it to warm up.

When the spaghetti squash is finished cooking, use a fork to gently scrape the insides to make spaghetti-like strings.

Place the spaghetti squash into each bowl along with the sauce. Garnish with the parsley.

# *Chicken* SALSA VERDE SOUP

If you're trying to cut carbs, this is the perfect soup for you! This protein-packed soup is fresh and a little spicy. And, trust me, you won't miss the noodles. Make sure to add the avocado, as fats help keep you full. I especially love Trader Joe's Salsa Verde because despite being in a jar, it tastes so fresh, and for someone who is sensitive to spicy foods, it has the perfect amount of heat.

**YIELD**: 4 servings
**TOTAL TIME**: 30 minutes

## INGREDIENTS

2 tbsp (30 ml) olive oil

**¼ yellow onion, diced**

Salt and pepper, to taste

1 tsp dried oregano

1 tsp dried basil

**1 (12-oz [340-g]) jar Trader Joe's Salsa Verde**

1 (32-oz [946-ml]) container Trader Joe's Organic Low Sodium Chicken Broth

**1 lb (454 g) chicken breasts**

**1 avocado, pitted and sliced**

**Jalapeño, sliced**

## DIRECTIONS

Add the olive oil to a large pot over medium heat. Add the onion, salt, pepper, oregano and basil and stir. Let it cook until the onion becomes translucent, 5 to 7 minutes.

Add the entire jar of salsa verde along with the entire container of chicken broth. When the liquid starts to bubble, add the chicken and cook for 25 minutes.

Take the chicken breasts out of the pot and shred them with two forks before adding it back to the pot.

To serve, add soup to four bowls and top with avocado and jalapeño slices.

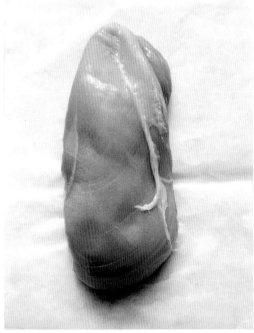

# *Fall* BRUSSELS SPROUTS AND QUINOA SALAD

This recipe is quick, easy, healthy and comforting, and it has all the sweet and savory flavors of fall. It can be served as a side, or add some chicken or tofu for a little extra protein! Trader Joe's Organic Balsamic & Fig Dressing is one of my favorites and pairs perfectly with this autumnal-inspired salad.

**YIELD**: 2 servings
**TOTAL TIME**: 15 minutes

## INGREDIENTS

1 (16-oz [454-g]) bag Brussels sprouts

½ cup (73 g) Trader Joe's Dried Cranberries (sugar-free)

½ cup (75 g) Trader Joe's Goat Cheese Crumbles

1 (8-oz [227-g]) packet Trader Joe's Fully Cooked Organic Quinoa

2 tbsp (30 ml) Trader Joe's Organic Balsamic & Fig Dressing

## DIRECTIONS

Microwave the Brussels sprouts in the packaging for 3 minutes. Carefully take them out of package and cut each into quarters. Add them to a large bowl.

Add the cranberries and goat cheese to the bowl and set aside.

Puncture the quinoa bag four or five times on the seam side, place it in the microwave seam side up and heat on high for 3½ minutes. Allow it to sit in the closed microwave for 2½ minutes.

Carefully remove the quinoa from the microwave, open it and pour it into the bowl with the other ingredients. Mix well.

Drizzle with the dressing and serve.

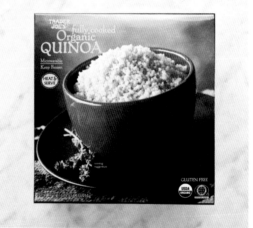

# *Creamy* ACAI SMOOTHIE BOWL

Trader Joe's Organic Acai Bowl is okay as is, but if you really want to take it up a notch, use this recipe. Yes, it's a few extra steps, but it takes this bowl from "meh" to "AYEEE!" (Which is a very good thing.)

**YIELD**: 1 smoothie bowl
**TOTAL TIME**: 5 minutes

## INGREDIENTS

1 (10-oz [284-g]) box of Trader Joe's Organic Acai Bowl

1 cup (240 ml) Trader Joe's Oat Beverage, plus more if needed

½ cup (62 g) raspberries

½ cup (74 g) blueberries

1 banana, sliced

## DIRECTIONS

Defrost the acai bowl overnight or microwave it for 2 minutes.

Place the contents of the bowl in a blender with the oat beverage and blend until smooth, adding more oat beverage until the desired consistency is reached.

Place the smoothie back in the bowl, and top it with the granola and coconut package that is included in the acai box, along with the raspberries, blueberries and banana.

# *Fresh and Spicy*
## TOFU BOWL

Tofu is a protein that I feel confuses non-vegetarians and people who did not grow up eating it. While I belong to neither of those categories, it is one of my favorite proteins. The pre-seasoned sriracha tofu from Trader Joe's makes life easier because there is no draining of the moisture involved, as well as no panfrying or broiling to get the right texture. In fact, you can eat this cold, saving you time and a headache.

**YIELD**: 2 servings
**TOTAL TIME**: 10 minutes

### INGREDIENTS

1 (10-oz [280-g]) pouch Trader Joe's Organic Jasmine Rice (microwavable)

1 (7-oz [198-g]) package Trader Joe's Sriracha Flavored Baked Tofu

1 avocado

2 cups (60 g) Trader Joe's Organic Power to the Greens salad mix

2 tbsp (57 g) Trader Joe's Kimchi

### DIRECTIONS

Microwave the jasmine rice for 3 minutes.

Cube the baked tofu.

Cut the avocado in half, take out the pit and then slice lengthwise and widthwise to cube.

Assemble the bowls by adding half the rice, half the cubed tofu, half the cubed avocado, 1 cup (30 g) of greens and 1 tablespoon (29 g) of kimchi to each.

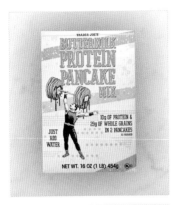

# *Blueberry* PROTEIN MUFFINS

Who doesn't love a blueberry muffin? I know I do! What I don't love though is how sugar-filled the ones at my favorite bakeries and coffee shops are. These muffins here are perfect in the morning with your coffee, especially because they are made with Trader Joe's protein pancake mix and sweetened with just a touch of maple syrup.

**YIELD**: 12 muffins
**TOTAL TIME**: 45 minutes

### INGREDIENTS

**2 cups (240 g) Trader Joe's Buttermilk Protein Pancake Mix**

**½ cup (120 ml) Trader Joe's 100% Pure Maple Syrup**

**1 egg**

**2 cups (480 ml) water or milk**

**1 cup (148 g) fresh blueberries**

### DIRECTIONS

Preheat the oven to 400°F (200°C). Line a 12-cup muffin tin with paper liners.

In a large mixing bowl, add the pancake mix, maple syrup, egg and water or milk. Stir with a whisk or large spoon until the mixture is smooth and there are no clumps.

Gently fold in the blueberries.

Pour the mixture into the muffin tin and bake for 15 minutes.

# Elevated Frozen Dinners

There are many things that separate Trader Joe's from other grocery stores, including the friendly staff, the seasonal goodies and their award-worthy frozen foods. Is there an award for frozen foods? If not, there should be. Now, of course we all know about the cult classic Mandarin Orange Chicken. We've been there, we've done that, we'll continue to do that, but there are so many underrated frozen meals that need to be talked about. Some of my favorites from this section include the Frozen Veggie Enchilada with the Fixins (page 105) and the Korean Beef Short Ribs Bowl (page 107). While the frozen items included are delicious all by themselves, the stars of the show are the sides that really bring all the flavors together.

# *Frozen* VEGGIE ENCHILADA WITH THE FIXINS

Ah, another meal I ate all the time my first two years of grad school. Brings back sweet, sweet memz. This enchilada is good on its own, but if you really love yourself, which I know you do, you should definitely add some avocado, eggs, cheese, cilantro and jalapeño to really take this baby up a notch. If you're truly in a pinch, you can microwave the enchilada, but I've had it both ways, and I swear by baking it in the oven.

**YIELD**: 1 serving
**TOTAL TIME**: 50 minutes

## INGREDIENTS

1 (9.5-oz [269-g]) package Trader Joe's Black Bean & Corn Enchilada

1 tbsp (15 ml) olive oil

**1 egg**

⅔ cup (75 g) Trader Joe's Fancy Shredded Mexican Style Cheese Blend

½ avocado, sliced

1 tbsp (15 ml) Trader Joe's Sour Cream

## DIRECTIONS

Preheat the oven to 350°F (180°C).

Remove the outer packaging from the enchilada and cover the tray it comes in with aluminum foil. Place it on the center rack of the oven and bake for 50 minutes.

After 45 minutes, add the olive oil to a skillet and place over medium heat. Fry the egg by cracking it into the skillet, flipping it once the white's set and cooking until the yolk reaches your desired doneness.

Once the enchilada is cooked, take it out of the oven and sprinkle the cheese on top. Add the fried egg, avocado slices and sour cream.

# *Korean* BEEF SHORT RIBS BOWL

Here is another unbelievably quick and high-quality meal for you to try. Trader Joe's has definitely helped make our lives easier by making these ribs super thinly cut and scrumptiously marinated. Add some chili onion crunch for spice and sprinkle with some cilantro for the perfect dinner.

**YIELD**: 4 servings
**TOTAL TIME**: 20 minutes

## INGREDIENTS

1 (20-oz [566-g]) package Trader Joe's Korean Style Beef Short Ribs

2 tbsp (30 ml) Trader Joe's Chili Onion Crunch, plus more as desired

1 tbsp (15 ml) olive oil

1 cup (110 g) green beans

Salt and pepper, as desired

2 (10-oz [280-g]) pouches Trader Joe's Organic Jasmine Rice (microwavable)

2 tbsp (57 g) Trader Joe's Kimchi

## DIRECTIONS

Thaw the short ribs by submerging the bag in cold water for 10 to 15 minutes. Remove the ribs from the bag before cooking.

Preheat a skillet or grill over medium-high heat. If you're using a skillet, cook each side of the ribs for 2 to 3 minutes until golden brown. If you're using a grill, grill until the meat is golden brown, 6 to 7 minutes. Brush about ½ tablespoon (8 ml) or more, as desired, of the chili onion crunch on each short rib.

Add the oil to a saucepan over medium heat, then add the green beans, salt and pepper, cover with a lid and stir occasionally until cooked through, 5 to 10 minutes (depending on how crunchy or soggy you like your green beans—I'm team soggy!).

Microwave each packet of rice separately for 3 minutes.

To assemble your short rib bowls, divide the rice, short ribs, green beans and kimchi between four bowls.

# *Meatball* PARMESAN SUB

The Italian Style Meatballs from Trader Joe's are so much better than your average frozen meatball. While I have shamelessly eaten these meatballs on their own, they are perfect in a meatball sub. Add some crunch by including Trader Joe's Gourmet Fried Onion Pieces.

**YIELD**: 4 servings
**TOTAL TIME**: 25 minutes

### INGREDIENTS

1 (16-oz [454-g]) package Trader Joe's Italian Style Meatballs

2½ cups (600 ml) Trader Joe's Roasted Garlic Marinara

1 Trader Joe's Organic French Baguette

8–12 slices Trader Joe's Sliced Provolone

4 tbsp (14 g) Trader Joe's Gourmet Fried Onion Pieces

### DIRECTIONS

Place the meatballs in a large saucepan over medium heat. Add the marinara and cook with the lid on until the meatballs are heated through, about 20 minutes.

Cut the baguette in half lengthwise. Add the meatballs to the baguette, then top with the cheese.

Broil the sandwiches in the oven on a foil-lined baking sheet until the cheese begins to bubble, about 3 minutes.

Take the baguette out of the oven and top with the onion pieces. Cut into four sandwiches and serve.

# *Fiocchetti* WITH PINK SAUCE AND SHRIMP

I can confidently say that this is my favorite frozen pasta product from Trader Joe's. The key to this pasta, however, is not following the directions on the bag. It calls for far too much oil and water. Follow the instructions below to make the fiocchetti with pink sauce of your dreams.

**YIELD**: 4 servings
**TOTAL TIME**: 10 minutes

## INGREDIENTS

1 tbsp (15 ml) olive oil

**1 (16-oz [454-g]) package Trader Joe's Cheese Filled Fiocchetti with Pink Sauce**

**1 cup (325 g) Trader Joe's Medium Cooked Shrimp, peeled and deveined, tail off**

**1 cup (30 g) spinach**

## DIRECTIONS

In a nonstick saucepan over medium heat, heat the olive oil.

Add the contents of the fiocchetti bag and the shrimp and heat for 6 to 7 minutes, stirring occasionally.

Add the spinach and stir until it wilts, about 3 minutes. Divide the fiocchetti among four bowls.

# CHICKEN AND EGG *Breakfast Biscuit*

I will admit that from time to time, I love visiting the drive-through of a certain fast food chain and ordering a chicken biscuit for breakfast. When I wanted to forego the shame of the employees knowing my name and order the second I said hello, I made my own version at home. These are just as good because the Trader Joe's biscuits taste nearly homemade, which, if you're a lover of homemade biscuits, you know is hard to come by. These little sandwiches are perfect for the whole fam.

**YIELD**: 8 biscuit sandwiches
**TOTAL TIME**: 35 minutes

## INGREDIENTS

1 (16-oz [454-g]) can Trader Joe's Buttermilk Biscuits

8 frozen Trader Joe's Breaded Chicken Tenderloin Breasts

4 eggs

Salt and pepper, as desired

2 tbsp (30 ml) milk

½ cup (120 ml) Trader Joe's 100% Pure Maple Syrup

## DIRECTIONS

Preheat the oven to 350°F (180°C). Line two baking sheets with aluminum foil.

Place the biscuits 2 inches (5 cm) apart on one baking sheet, and bake on the middle rack for 16 to 18 minutes.

Remove the biscuits from the oven and turn up the temperature to 425°F (220°C). Place the chicken on the second baking sheet and bake for 12 to 15 minutes.

While the tenders are baking, in a large bowl whisk together the eggs, salt, pepper and milk. Add the egg mixture to a saucepan over medium heat and scramble until the eggs reach your desired doneness, about 5 minutes for firm and fully cooked eggs.

Assemble the breakfast biscuits by placing some egg, a chicken tenderloin and a drizzle of maple syrup in between each biscuit.

# *Pittsburgh-Style* BURGER

A few years ago, I visited Pittsburgh for the wedding of a dear friend. Before the festivities began, my husband and I decided to explore the city, which meant eating a lot. We stopped by a restaurant famous for its french-fry-filled sandwiches and burgers. I was floored by how simple but delicious our meals were. I simply cannot wait to go back, but until then, I make this Pittsburgh-style burger about once a month. I add my own Trader Joe's spin to the burger by using Magnifisauce instead of the dressing that comes in the coleslaw mixture. Trust me on this one!

**YIELD**: 4 hamburgers
**TOTAL TIME**: 35 minutes

## INGREDIENTS

1 (1½-lb [680-g]) package Trader Joe's Potato Fries

1 lb (454 g) Trader Joe's Grass Fed Angus Beef

1 (10-oz [284-g]) package Trader Joe's Organic Coleslaw Kit

¼ cup (60 ml) Trader Joe's Magnifisauce

8 slices white bread

## DIRECTIONS

Preheat the oven to 425°F (220°C). Lightly coat a baking sheet with nonstick cooking spray.

Arrange the fries in a single layer on the baking sheet. Cook for 14 minutes.

Heat a grill or a skillet over medium-high heat. Form the ground beef into four patties, then sear them on both sides, about 2 minutes each, and continue cooking them until your desired temperature is reached. The internal temperature should be about 150°F (65°C) for a medium-cooked burger or 160°F (70°C) for well done.

Place the coleslaw (but not the dressing that came in the package!) in a medium bowl and toss with the Magnifisauce.

Assemble the burger by placing each atop a slice of bread, and then add the coleslaw and fries. Top with a second slice of bread.

# *Carnitas* NACHOS WITH PLANTAIN CHIPS

Trader Joe's Plantain Chips are perfect. Just the right amount of salt, crunch and, yeah, I'll say it, greasiness to satisfy all of your savory food cravings. So, I thought to myself, Why not go the extra mile and make nachos using plantain crisps instead of tortilla chips?! This was one of my best cooking ideas in a while.

**YIELD**: 4 servings
**TOTAL TIME**: 15 minutes

## INGREDIENTS

1 (12-oz [340-g]) package Trader Joe's Traditional Carnitas

1 (5-oz [142-g]) bag Trader Joe's Plantain Chips

1 cup (113 g) Trader Joe's Fancy Shredded Mexican Style Cheese Blend

½ cup (120 g) Trader Joe's Chunky Spicy Guacamole Auténtico

⅔ cup (143 g) Trader Joe's Salsa Especial

## DIRECTIONS

Preheat the oven to 450°F (230°C). Line a baking sheet with aluminum foil.

Place the carnitas in a microwave-safe bowl and microwave for 2 to 3 minutes, and then shred them with a fork.

Place all of the plantain chips in the bag onto the baking sheet and sprinkle with the carnitas and cheese. Bake until the cheese starts to bubble, about 5 minutes.

Take the baking sheet out of the oven and add dollops of guacamole and Salsa Especial.

# SPAGHETTI AND *Meatballs*

If there's one thing you need to know about me it's that I love a marinara sauce. When I have time, I like to cook things low and slow, developing the flavor over time with lots of ingredients. But, more often than not, I don't have the time, so I cut a few corners using ingredients like anchovies (controversial, I know) to help me get all that depth of flavor in a short amount of time. Trust me, you will love this sauce!

**YIELD**: 4 servings
**TOTAL TIME**: 45 minutes

### INGREDIENTS

1 tbsp (15 ml) olive oil

**1 shallot, peeled and sliced**

**2 anchovies**

**1 (18-oz [510-g]) jar Trader Joe's Traditional Marinara Sauce**

**1 (16-oz [454-g]) package Trader Joe's Italian Style Meatballs**

2 tbsp (28 g) salt

**1 (16-oz [454-g]) package Trader Joe's Italian Spaghetti**

### DIRECTIONS

Place a medium pot over medium heat. Add the olive oil and shallot and cook until the shallot becomes caramelized, 7 to 8 minutes.

Add the anchovies and break them up with a wooden spoon. Stir and combine, and cook for 3 to 5 minutes.

Add the jar of marinara sauce to the pot, let it come to a simmer, and then add the meatballs. Place a lid on top and heat for 20 minutes.

In a large pot, bring 4 quarts (4 L) of water to a boil. Add the salt and spaghetti. Boil for 8 minutes, stirring frequently. Drain the pasta and add it directly to the sauce and meatballs. Stir together and serve.

# *Breakfast* PIZZA

The tarte D'Alsace with ham, caramelized onions and gruyere cheese is the best pizza Trader Joe's has. Hands down. Unfortunately, one pizza is only filling enough for a single adult. To bulk up this delicious and flaky pizza, add an egg and some arugula for good measure.

**YIELD**: 2 servings
**TOTAL TIME**: 20 minutes

## INGREDIENTS

1 (8-oz [227-g]) box Maître Pierre Tarte D'Alsace

2 eggs

1 cup (30 g) arugula

## DIRECTIONS

Preheat the oven to 450°F (230°C). Line a baking sheet with aluminum foil.

Place the pizza on the baking sheet and bake for 10 minutes.

Crack the eggs on the pizza and sprinkle the arugula on top.

Cook for 7 minutes.

# Sweet Tooth

This section is quite ironically titled "Sweet Tooth" because your girl (me) actually could live without sweets. That being said, these recipes are my go-tos when I am craving something ooey, gooey, sweet and delicious. Also, they're incredibly easy to make! My favorites are the Chocolate Chip Cookies with Caramel Filling (page 131) and the Sticky Apple Coffee Cake (page 135).

# *Chocolate-Topped* PUMPKIN BREAD

Fall is truly the most wonderful time of the year. My birthday is in October. My husband's birthday is in October. WE GOT MARRIED ON HALLOWEEN, PEOPLE! I love the fall! When the leaves start to turn brown (and even before that, really), I begin making pumpkin bread. Follow the simple directions on the box, but elevate it by adding semi-sweet chocolate chips.

**YIELD**: 12–15 slices
**TOTAL TIME**: 70 minutes

## INGREDIENTS

**2 large eggs**

½ cup (120 ml) vegetable oil

**1 (17.5-oz [496-g]) Trader Joe's Pumpkin Bread & Muffin Mix**

**½ cup (84 g) Trader Joe's Semi-Sweet Chocolate Chips**

(continued)

# *Chocolate-Topped* PUMPKIN BREAD (CONTINUED)

## DIRECTIONS

Preheat the oven to 350°F (180°C). Lightly grease a 9 x 5–inch (23 x 13–cm) loaf pan with butter or cooking spray.

In a medium bowl, combine the eggs, oil and 1 cup (240 ml) of water. Add the bread mix and fold together the ingredients with a rubber spatula until the batter is smooth, 1 to 2 minutes.

Spread the batter in the loaf pan, filling the corners and leveling the top.

Pour the semi-sweet chocolate chips over the mix. Alternatively, you can add the chips in with the mix, but it looks prettier on top.

Bake for 60 minutes and allow to cool for 15 minutes before removing from the pan.

# *Chocolate* CHIP COOKIES WITH CARAMEL FILLING

This recipe is especially for all my gluten-free friends out there! It's also for their friends, who are sometimes forced to eat gluten-free goodies, which, let's be honest, aren't always as good as gluten-filled treats. The caramel in these cookies adds some much-needed moisture and creaminess to these almond flour chocolate chip cookies. I could eat these on the regular!

**YIELD**: 12 cookies
**TOTAL TIME**: 30 minutes

## INGREDIENTS

2 tbsp (30 ml) melted salted butter or vegetable oil

2 tsp (10 ml) vanilla extract

1 (9.4-oz [266-g]) package Trader Joe's Almond Flour Chocolate Chip Cookie Baking Mix

3 tbsp (45 ml) dairy or non-dairy milk

4 Trader Joe's Fleur de Sel Caramels pieces

## DIRECTIONS

Preheat the oven to 350°F (180°C). Line a baking sheet with parchment paper, or grease it.

In a medium bowl, mix the butter or oil and vanilla extract until creamy.

Add the baking mix and stir to incorporate.

Add the milk, 1 tablespoon (15 ml) at a time, until the dough comes together.

With your hands or a cookie scoop, make roughly 1-ounce (28-g) balls that are about 1 inch (2.5 cm) in diameter.

Cut the caramels into thirds and place one-third of a caramel into the middle of each ball. Roll the ball in your hands and make sure the caramel is covered with the dough.

Place the balls of dough 2 inches (5 cm) apart on the baking sheet and bake for 14 minutes. Let the cookies rest on the baking sheet for 2 minutes before transferring them with a spatula to a cooling rack to cool completely.

# *Chocolate* CHIP COOKIES WITH CARAMEL FILLING (CONTINUED)

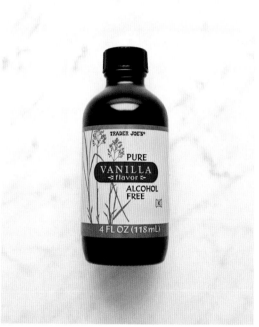

# *Sticky* APPLE COFFEE CAKE

The coffee cake from a certain popular chain is probably my favorite thing ever to have with coffee. Trader Joe's Cinnamon Crumb Coffee Cake in a box is just as good, in my opinion. If you can believe it, it gets even better by adding sliced apples to the bottom of the baking pan! It caramelizes and gets sticky and delicious. It's a perfectly indulgent breakfast treat!

**YIELD**: 8 servings
**TOTAL TIME**: 70 minutes

## INGREDIENTS

**1 (22-oz [624-g]) box Trader Joe's Cinnamon Crumb Coffee Cake Mix**

**⅔ cup (160 ml) milk or water**

**1 egg**

6 tbsp (90 ml) melted butter or vegetable oil

2 tbsp (28 g) cubed unsalted butter

**Pink Lady apple, sliced**

(continued)

# *Sticky* APPLE COFFEE CAKE (CONTINUED)

## DIRECTIONS

Preheat the oven to 350°F (180°C). Butter and lightly flour a 9-inch (23-cm) round or square cake pan.

In a large bowl, whisk together the cake mix (not the crumb mix), milk or water, egg and melted butter or vegetable oil. Do not overmix.

In a small bowl, add the cubed butter and the crumb mix from the cake mix box, and use your hands to work together the butter and crumb mixture until little balls of sugar form.

Add the crumb and butter mixture evenly to the bottom of the cake pan, and then place the apple slices on top (these do not have to be uniform).

Pour the cake mixture on top. It will be thick, so you will have to spread it around with a spatula to even it out.

Bake for 50 minutes. Let it cool for 10 minutes before you flip it over onto a plate so the apples are on top.

# *No-Bake* CHOCOLATE-COVERED COCONUT CLUSTERS

Baking used to be extremely intimidating for me. I mean, we all heard, "Baking is a science!" in our middle school home ec classes. Since baking is a little less intuitive than I like, I tend to stay away from it. Those of you who feel the same way will get a bit of relief from these no-bake chocolate-covered coconut clusters! Because there are no eggs in them, you can taste and see if they're flavored to your liking without worrying about salmonella. The only thing you do have to worry about is finishing them in five minutes because they are that delicious—trust me.

**YIELD**: 6 servings
**TOTAL TIME**: 25 minutes

## INGREDIENTS

1 (8-oz [227-g]) package Trader Joe's Organic Unsweetened Flake Coconut

3 tbsp plus 1 tsp (50 ml) melted coconut oil, divided

2 tbsp (30 ml) Trader Joe's 100% Pure Maple Syrup

1 tsp vanilla extract

¼ cup (42 g) Trader Joe's Semi-Sweet Chocolate Chips

## DIRECTIONS

In a food processor or blender, add the entire package of shredded coconut, 3 tablespoons (45 ml) of the melted coconut oil, the maple syrup and vanilla extract. Pulse the mixture until it begins to stick together.

With your hands, form the mixture into 1- to 1½-inch (2.5- to 4-cm) balls.

In a saucepan over very low heat, add the chocolate chips and remaining coconut oil. Stir until melted.

Drizzle the melted chocolate over the coconut clusters. Put them in the fridge, uncovered, for 5 to 10 minutes to let the chocolate solidify before serving.

# *Cookies and Cream* CAKE

When I was a child, you could not pry a cookies-and-cream candy bar from my tiny little fingers. I loved those things! These days, white chocolate tends to be a little too sweet for me (I have a notorious "salt tooth"), but this cake gives me that perfect vanilla-y cookie taste that I crave from my childhood.

**YIELD**: 9 cake slices
**TOTAL TIME**: 50 minutes

## INGREDIENTS

1 stick plus 2 tbsp (150 ml) melted butter

**2 eggs**

**2 cups (480 ml) milk**

**1 (16-oz [454-g]) box Trader Joe's Vanilla Cake & Baking Mix**

**10 Trader Joe's Joe-Joe's cookies**

## DIRECTIONS

Preheat the oven to 350°F (180°C), and grease a 9 x 9–inch (23 x 23–cm) baking dish.

In a bowl, whisk together the melted butter, eggs and milk until creamy and smooth.

Pour the cake mix into the mixture in ½-cup (120-g) increments, whisking to prevent clumping.

With your hands, crumble the Joe Joe's over the cake batter and combine.

Pour the cake batter into the baking dish and bake for 35 to 40 minutes.

# *Cornbread* BLUEBERRY COBBLER

This blueberry cobbler is super simple to make. Just fold in blueberries into the cornbread mixture. I love the cornbread mix from Trader Joe's because it is sweet on its own and crumbly without being dry. Although not a part of the official five ingredients, I would recommend serving with ice cream or whipped cream if you have some handy!

**YIELD**: 9 servings
**TOTAL TIME**: 50 minutes

## INGREDIENTS

**1 egg**
½ cup (120 ml) vegetable oil
**¾ cup (180 ml) milk**
**1 (15-oz [425-g]) box Trader Joe's Cornbread Mix**
**1 cup (148 g) blueberries**

## DIRECTIONS

Preheat the oven to 350°F (180°C). Grease an 8 x 8 x 2-inch (20 x 20 x 5-cm) baking dish.

In a large mixing bowl, beat the egg, oil and milk. Add the cornbread mix and stir until moistened, but do not overmix.

Pour the batter into the pan, and then add the blueberries on top of the batter.

Bake for 35 to 40 minutes.

# CANNOLI *Dip*

Nothing makes me happier than a cannoli. I kid you not! Even just the word makes my face light up. They're hard to make from home if you don't have a deep fryer, or patience to make the shell from scratch. So, cannoli dip is the second best thing, and it is just as delicious! Make it for guests for an instant hit.

**YIELD**: 4 servings
**TOTAL TIME**: 10 minutes

## INGREDIENTS

1 cup (246 g) Trader Joe's Whole Milk or Part Skim Ricotta Cheese

1 cup (224 g) Mascarpone Cheese

2 cups (240 g) Trader Joe's Powdered Cane Sugar

1 cup (168 g) Trader Joe's Semi-Sweet Chocolate Chips

1 (3.66-oz [104-g]) box Trader Joe's French Crêpe Wafer Cookies

## DIRECTIONS

In a large bowl, add the ricotta, mascarpone and powdered sugar. Whip with an electric mixer on medium speed until fluffy and well combined, about 5 minutes.

With a spatula, gently fold in the chocolate chips.

Place in a serving bowl and serve with the French Crêpe Wafer Cookies.

# Acknowledgments

I started my Instagram, @traceyjoes, for fun in the fall of 2019. Never did I think I would get to publish my very own cookbook! I have many people to thank, including my sweet husband, David, who is my biggest cheerleader and the first @traceyjoes follower. David has patiently sat by while his food gets cold as I attempt to take the most Instagram-worthy photos. When he wanted to do Whole30 in January to get back on track after the holidays, I told him it would help me if he didn't because it was recipe-testing time. He generously sacrificed his waistline for me by tasting each creation and letting me know what he thought.

I also want to thank my dad and brother for their support, but especially my mother for her inspiration. Whenever I came home from college and grad school, she always had my favorite foods lined up. I was very spoiled, and I never had to learn how to cook until my mid-twenties, but now that I know how, my cooking shines with her love.

I also want to thank my in-laws for being Tracey Joe's supporters and bragging about me to all of their friends and family ☺. I want to thank all of my friends, especially Heather, who helped me come up with the name "Tracey Joe's." While it all seems so obvious now, I was thinking of Instagram names for about a month until she basically said "TRACEY JOE'S, DUH!" So, thanks girl, PPL.

I also want to acknowledge my generous and patient editor, Marissa. I know I don't always follow directions that well or write super clearly on the first go-round, but I truly appreciate your comments and suggestions for this book! I'd like to thank my copy editor, Joe Rhatigan, who made this book read smooth like butter, people!

# About the Author

Tracey is the creator of the @traceyjoes Instagram account. She moonlights as a home chef, but her day job is in academia. She somehow managed to write this cookbook as she finished her dissertation. Both were labors of love.

# Index